Tam Taps!

By Sally Cowan

I am Tam.

I tip ... I tap!

3

Tam taps.

Tip, tap!

Tap, tip!

Pip is at the mat.

Pip sits.

Tam taps.

CHECKING FOR MEANING

1. What did Tam do? *(Literal)*

2. Where did Pip go? *(Literal)*

3. Why didn't Pip like Tam's new hobby? *(Inferential)*

EXTENDING VOCABULARY

am	Look at the word *am*. How many sounds are in the word? Use *am* in a sentence about yourself.
Tip	Look at the word *Tip*. What does *Tip* mean in this story? What else can the word *Tip* mean?
taps	Look at the word *taps*. What is the base of this word? What has been added to the base? Find another example of a word in the book that has *s* added to the base.

MOVING BEYOND THE TEXT

1. What could Tam do to help Pip get used to her new hobby?

2. Do you think tap dancing is a good hobby? Why or why not?

3. What are your hobbies?

4. What are some other hobbies people have? Which ones are quiet and which ones are loud?

SPEED SOUNDS

Mm	Ss	Aa	Pp	Ii	Tt

am

Tam

tip

sit

Sit

tap

at

Pip

taps

sits

mat